Page 9

Page 11

Page 13

Page 15

Page 17

Page 19

Page 21

Page 23

Page 25

Page 27

Page 29

Page 31

Page 33

Page 35

Page 37

Page 39

Page 41

Page 43

Page 45

Page 47

Page 49

Page 51

Page 53

Page 5

Page 57

Page 59

Page 61

Page 6

Page 65

Page 67

Page 69

Page 7

Page 73

Page 75

Page 77

Page 7

Page 81

Page 83

Page 85

Page 8

COLOR-BY-NUMBER

COLOR-BY-NUMBER

THUNDER BAY
P · R · E · S · S

San Diego, California

Thunder Bay Press
An imprint of Printers Row Publishing Group
9717 Pacific Heights Blvd., San Diego, CA 92121
www.thunderbaybooks.com • mail@thunderbaybooks.com

Printers Row Publishing Group is a division of Readerlink Distribution Services, LLC.
Thunder Bay Press is a registered trademark of Readerlink Distribution Services, LLC.

Correspondence regarding the content of this book should be sent to Thunder Bay Press, Editorial Department, at the above address.

Thunder Bay Press
Publisher: Peter Norton
Associate Publisher: Ana Parker
Art Director: Charles McStravick
Senior Developmental Editor: Diane Cain
Senior Project Editor: Jessica Matteson
Editorial Assistant: Sarah Hillberg
Production Team: Beno Chan, Mimi Oey

Line Art: Carolyn Saletto

Produced by Judy O Productions, Inc.

ISBN: 978-1-6672-0181-8

Printed in China

27 26 25 24 23   1 2 3 4 5

In less than thirty minutes, with a blank canvas and just

a handful of colors on a palette, Bob Ross created beautiful works

of art week after week for his public television audience. From

magnificent mountains to striking seascapes, Bob demonstrated

the beauty in nature—and best of all, he showed that

ANYONE CAN CREATE ART!

The Joy of Painting first aired in January 1983 and continued for an incredible 403 episodes. Each week, Bob taught the techniques of painting, shared his joy for nature and all its little critters, and imparted wisdom and life advice with his unforgettably kind and encouraging words. Bob made it a point while filming to speak as though he were talking to just one person, and that one-on-one delivery is why so many viewers feel a special connection to him to this day.

Because Bob believed that anyone can be an artist, interpreting his masterpieces as color-by-number and creating art is the perfect way to spend the day! The coloring pages in this book feature line art expertly adapted from Bob's paintings on *The Joy of Painting*. From cabins and rivers to forests and oceans—and of course happy little clouds—you'll color each beautiful detail to bring Bob's landscapes and seascapes to life.

Creating art is as easy as one, two, three when you color by number with your favorite set of pencils or markers. Using the fold-out Color Key in the back of the book as your guide, match the numbers to their colors and begin filling in the spaces to see the art take shape. The Color Key makes it easy to find the perfect shade of greens for the trees and grass, blues for the skies, and yellows and oranges for the sunsets that Bob is known for.

The finished images of all 92 coloring pages are printed on the inside covers for easy reference. And all the pages in the book are perforated, so once your masterpieces are complete, carefully tear the pages out to display or gift and share the joy of painting with others.

Happy Coloring!

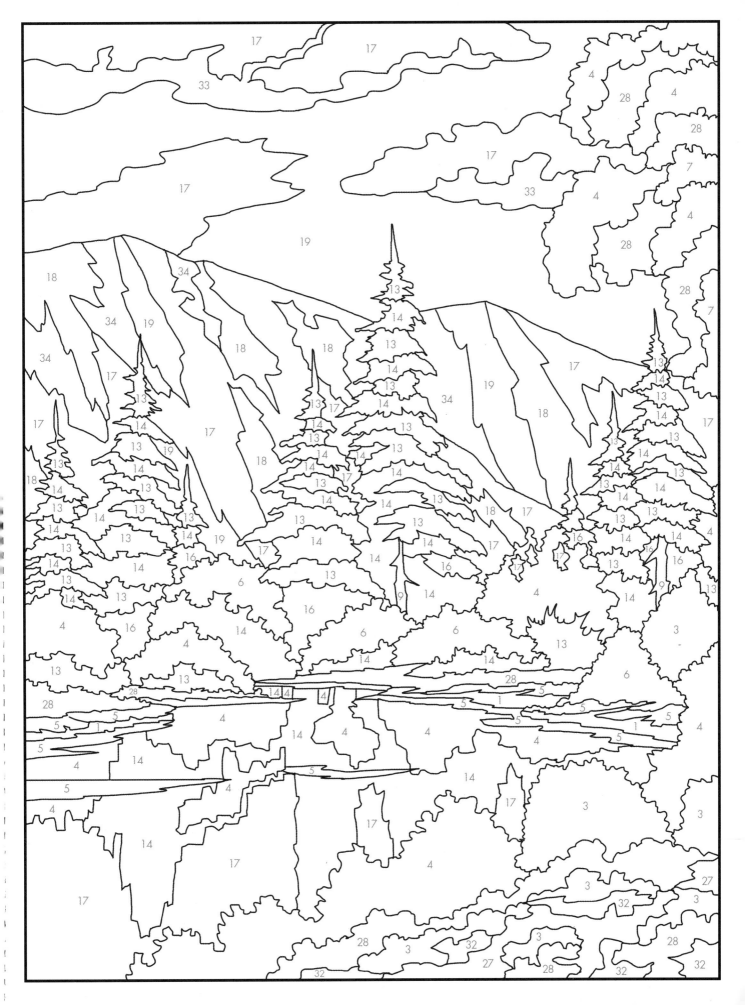

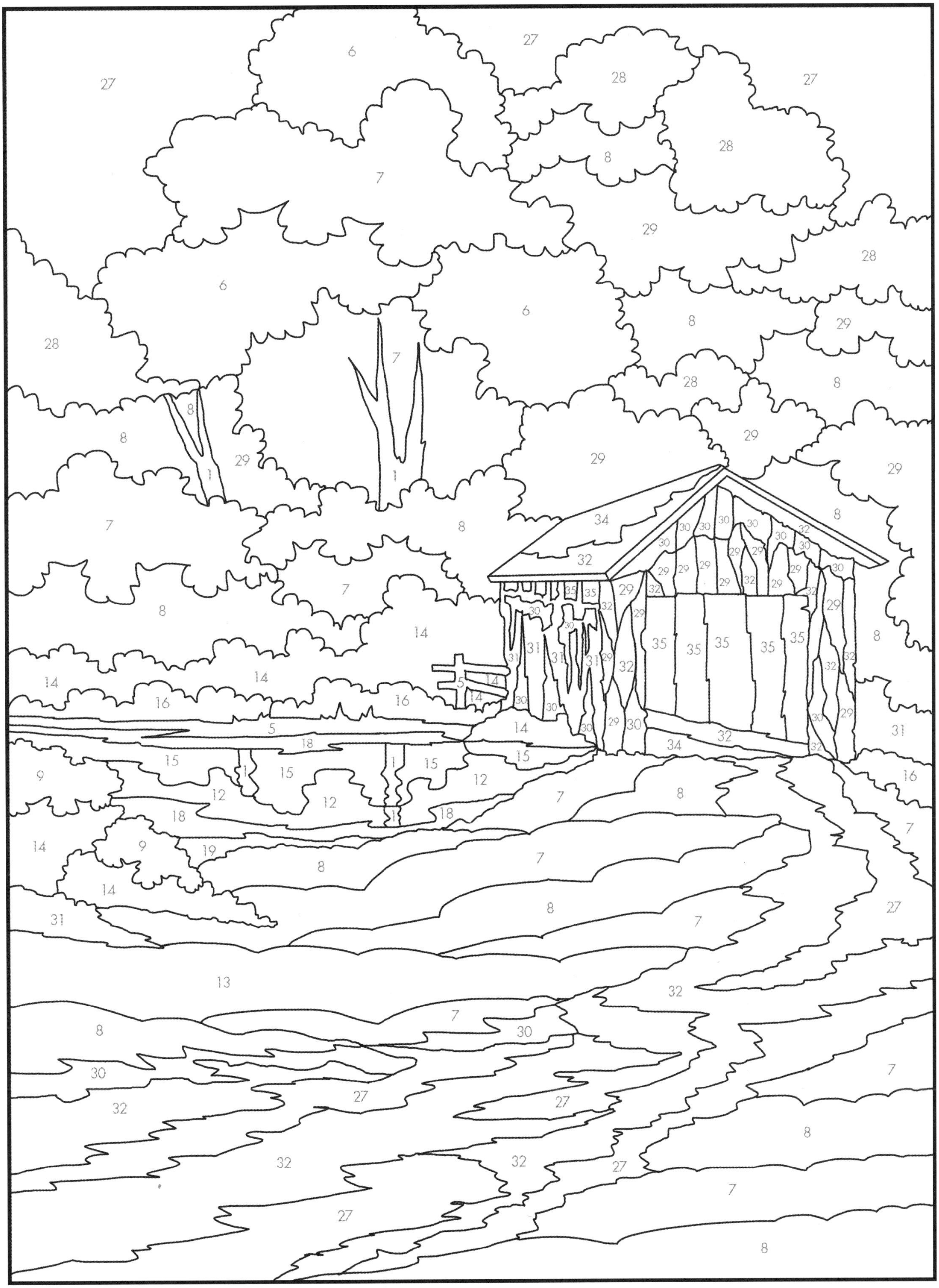

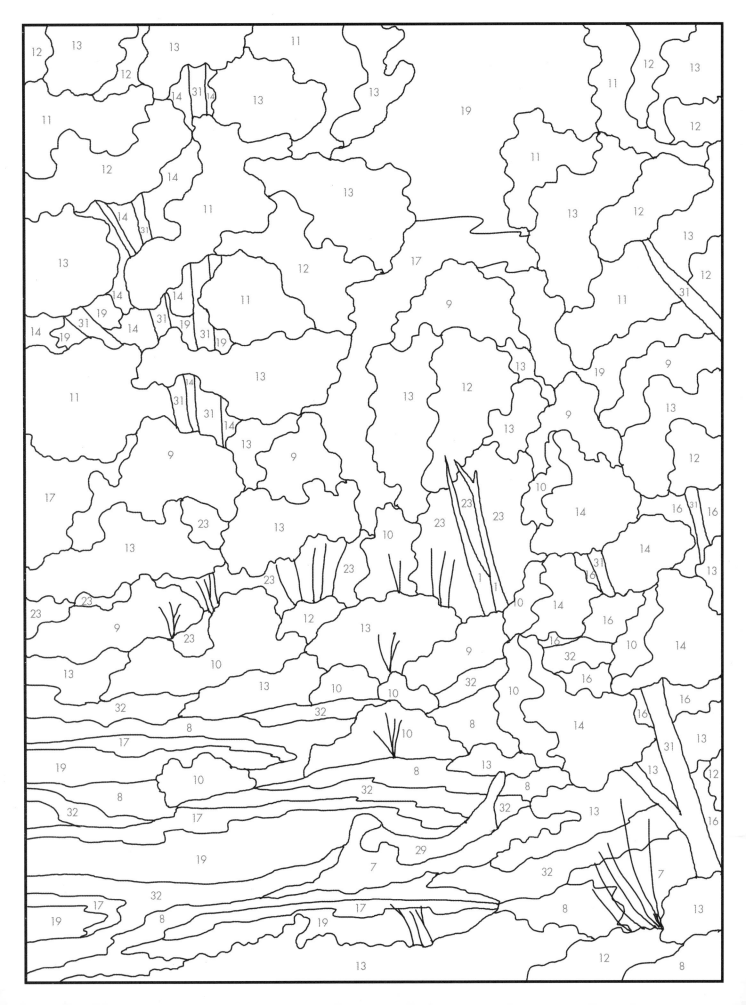

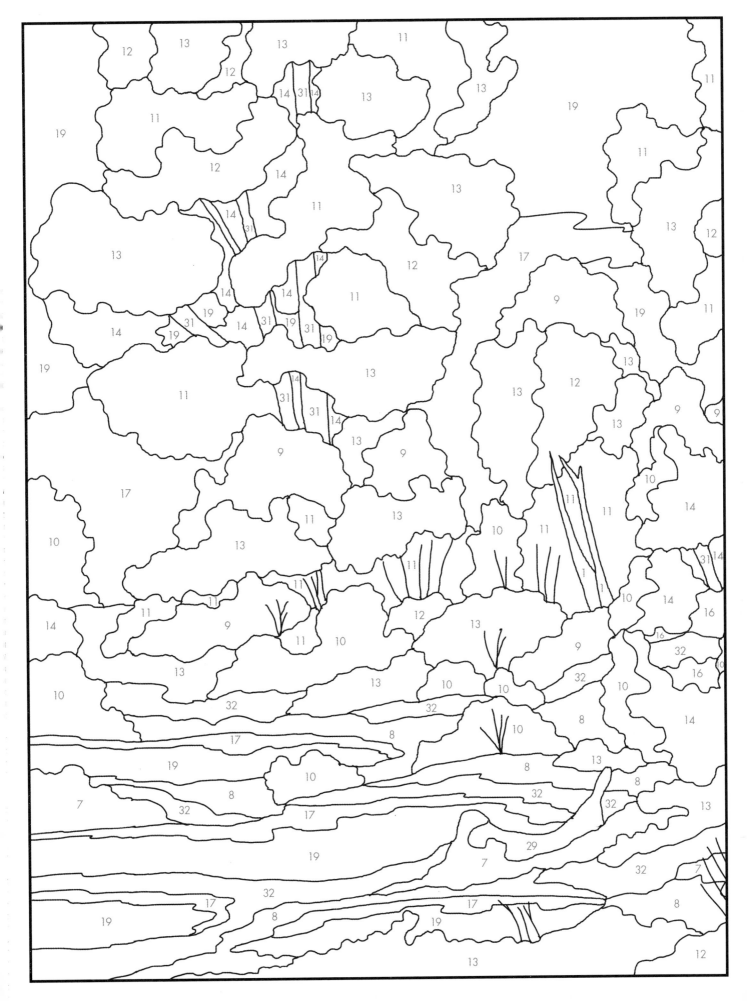

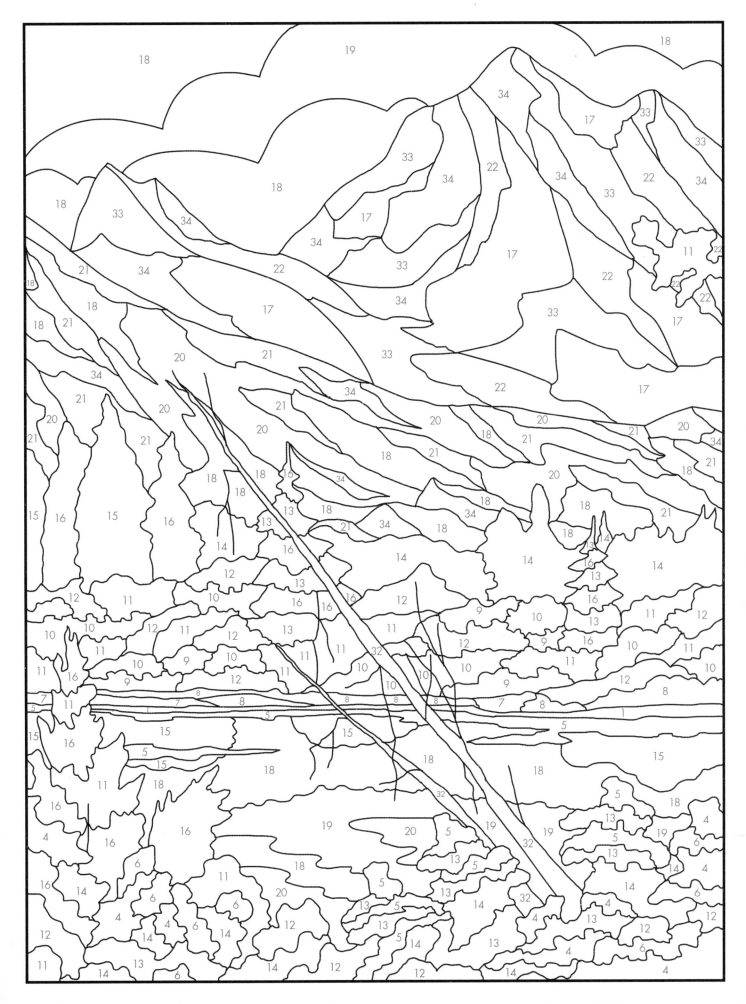

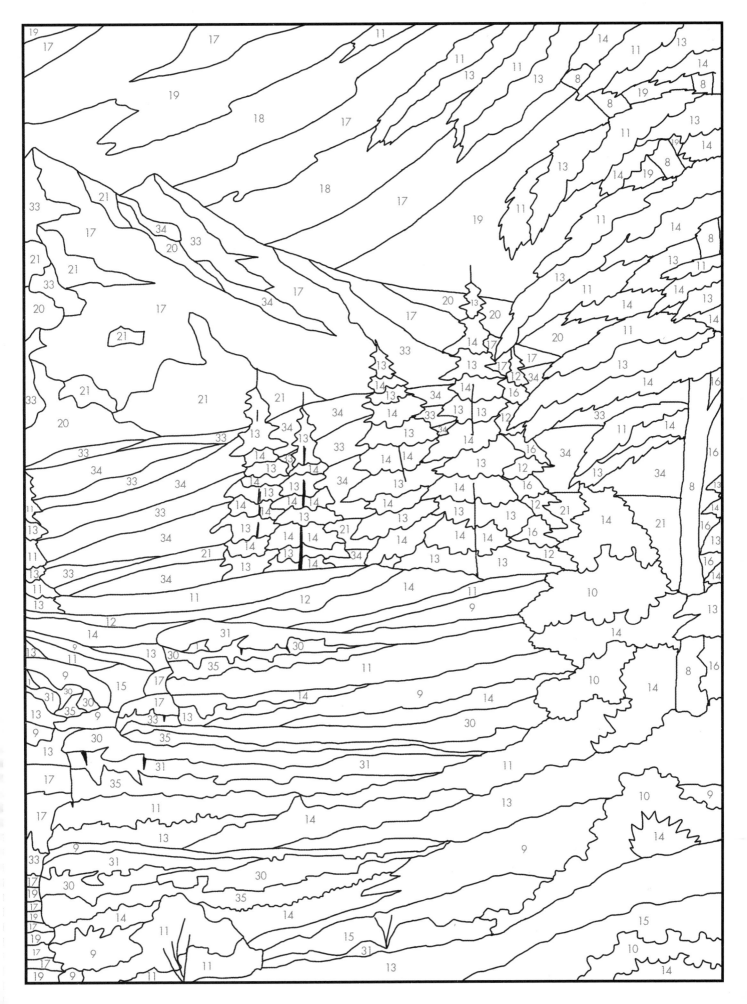

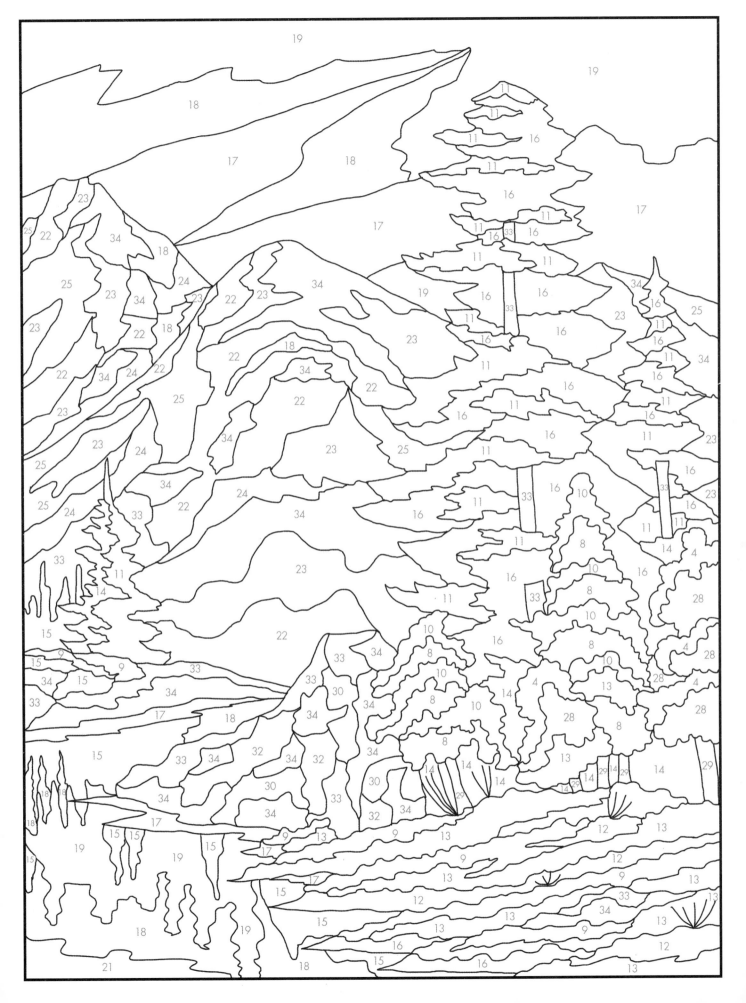

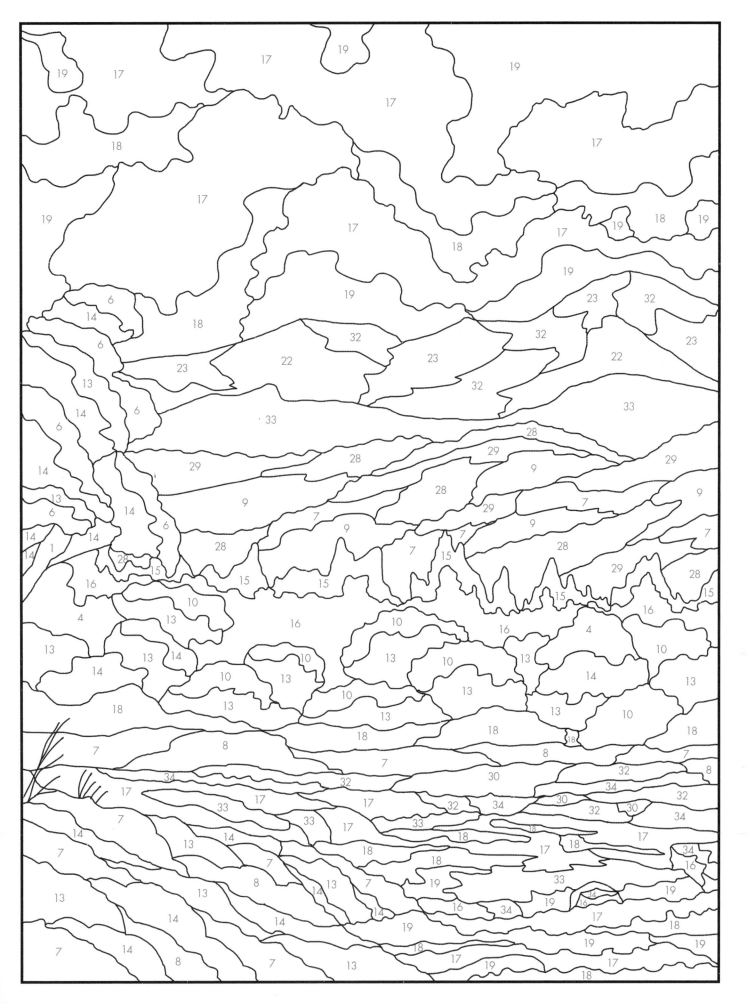